Watching the Watsonville Wetlands

Watching the Watsonville Wetlands

AN ARMCHAIR GUIDE TO THE WATSONVILLE SLOUGH SYSTEM

By Jerry Busch

Published by Watsonville Wetlands Watch
P.O. Box 1239
Freedom, California 95019-1239

FIRST EDITION
ISBN 0-9679463-0-1
Library of Congress

ACKNOWLEDGEMENTS

THIS BOOK WAS MADE POSSIBLE BY THE GENEROSITY
OF THE FOLLOWING ORGANIZATIONS AND INDIVIDUALS

The Wallis Foundation, The Lee-Kahn Foundation,
The Nicholson Family Trust, Patagonia,
County of Santa Cruz Fish and Game Advisory Commission,
The Compton Foundation, West Marine, Eschaton Foundation,
The Santa Cruz Regional Group of the Ventana Chapter Sierra Club,
Santa Cruz Surfrider Foundation, The Elkhorn Slough Foundation,
Campaign to Save Pajaro Valley Farmlands and Wetlands

Kathryn Metz, Diane Porter Cooley, Richard and Georgia Faggioli,
Pat and Roland Rebele, Cara Disimone, Julie and Robert Edwards,
Dave and Dorsa Walworth, Marilyn Sachs, Mary Marcus, Ed Frost,
Bill and Joyce Paterson, Barbara Graves, Amy Newell, Marian Martinez,
Bernie Feldman, and the general membership of Watsonville Wetlands Watch.

Rumsen Ohlone Song
(as given by Patrick Orozco's great uncle)

Rat Sings to Rabbit, Jack Rabbit, and Quail

Kai-stun
I dream

ka-mas
I dream of you

ex-lu-ya-xl
So dance

we-re-ne-kai
Rabbit

tce-ica-kai
Jack rabbit

ek-sena-kai
Dance quail

TABLE OF CONTENTS

ILLUSTRATOR

Andrea Rich

PHOTOGRAPHERS

Frank C. Maxey: page 28

Virginia Newton: pages 1, 6

Gypsy P. Ray: pages 34, 38, 46, 56, Back Cover

Edison Rosser: Front Cover, page 12

Victor Schiffrin: page 6

Carol Whitehill: page 80

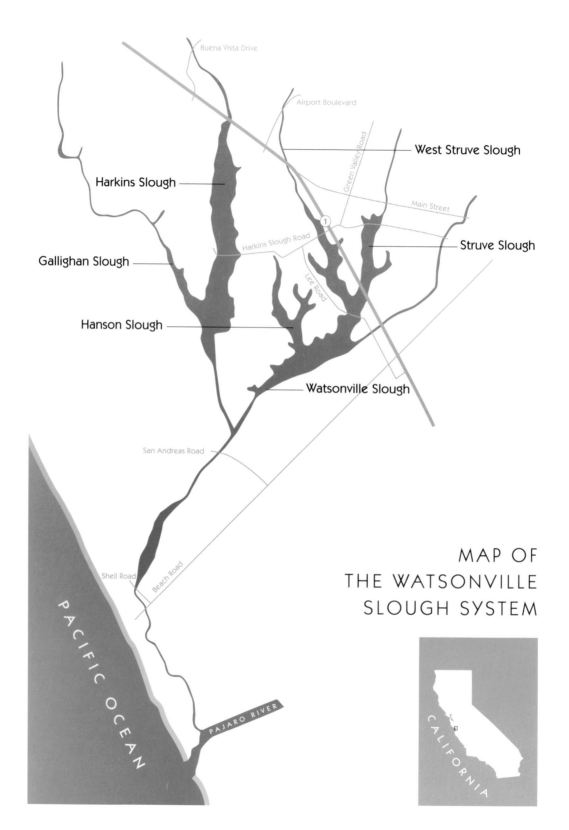

Buena Vista Drive

Airport Boulevard

West Struve Slough

Harkins Slough

Green Valley Road

Main Street

Gallighan Slough

Struve Slough

Harkins Slough Road

Lee Road

Hanson Slough

Watsonville Slough

San Andreas Road

MAP OF
THE WATSONVILLE
SLOUGH SYSTEM

Shell Road

Beach Road

PACIFIC OCEAN

PAJARO RIVER

CALIFORNIA

PREFACE

The six interlinked, freshwater sloughs that comprise the Watsonville Slough System lie at the southern end of Santa Cruz County, California, and are fed by the waters of the Pajaro Valley watershed. Adjacent to the city of Watsonville, the sloughs cover about 800 acres. The life in the uplands of the sloughs is so rich a food source that more species of migrating raptors are to be found here than at the larger, saltwater slough, Elkhorn Slough, just a few miles south in Monterey County. From Highway One, most of the Watsonville Sloughs are hidden. They wind around farms, fields, and low hills not visible from the highway. Access points to the sloughs are not marked on most maps, which makes them difficult to find.

California has lost over 90 percent of its wetlands to development, and the Watsonville Sloughs—one of the largest remaining freshwater marshlands in the state's coastal zone—provide a crucial resting place for many species of migrating birds. Among the thousands of birds and other abundant wildlife frequenting the sloughs are a variety of rare, threatened, and endangered species, including 27 of the 73 declining birds listed in California as "Species of Special Concern."

This book is intended to help people find and enjoy this endangered natural treasure. Gary Kittleson, a local hydrological consultant who has studied the formation of the sloughs, has summarized their geological history. Christine Johnson-Lyons, a founding member of the Watsonville Wetlands Watch, has written a brief social/cultural history of the area. Jerry Busch, a local writer and naturalist who has been observing these sloughs for two decades, has contributed the nature essays describing current life in the sloughs. These narratives were first published in the Watsonville Wetlands Watch newsletter, under the heading of "Slough Niches." The essays are organized so that each section focuses on one slough and is accompanied by maps with public access points noted on each map.

Andrea Rich, a nationally known nature artist who lives in Santa Cruz County, has created the fine woodcuts that illustrate the narratives. Gypsy Ray, a photographer and teacher at Cabrillo College, organized several photo shoots around the sloughs, which produced the photos contained in this book. Gypsy's students and professional colleagues collaborated in the shoots, and all the participants donated these photos, which capture well the beauty of this landscape.

We are especially indebted to Noreen Parks, a science writer and editor. Not only was she the copy editor for the book, she also joined our book committee and contributed many hours of her time researching crucial information and helping us negotiate the maze of the publication processes.

The mission of the Watsonville Wetlands Watch is to "protect, restore and appreciate the wetlands of the Pajaro Valley." It is our hope that people will use the information in the book for a first-hand exploration of the area and that it will deepen the pleasure and knowledge of those who already know the sloughs. We hope also that some of you readers will join us in restoring and protecting this irreplaceable part of our natural heritage.

—*The Book Committee for Watsonville Wetlands Watch: Noreen Parks, Caroline Rodgers, Ellie Van Houten, Mary Warshaw, and Carol Whitehill.*

Geology and Hydrology
of the Watsonville Sloughs

The rolling hills, green wetlands, and calm waters that make up the Watsonville Slough System are deceptive. A casual observer might imagine that the sloughs are just flat, shallow depressions on an otherwise uneventful terrain. They appear smooth and softened by a history of erosion and farming. Today one can drive by the sloughs and barely see them as flashes of green between the berry fields and the shopping centers. What lies below these marshes, however, is a complex story—a story driven by the slow, steady power of water, waves, wind, and tides on a geologically unstable, tectonically active coast.

To understand how the sloughs came to be, one must consider the recent geological history of the Monterey Bay region. About 11 million years ago, during the early Pliocene epoch, the San Joaquin Valley of Central California is believed to have drained through what we now recognize as the lower Pajaro, Elkhorn Slough, and Salinas River basins. As regional tectonic activity uplifted the coastal areas and Santa Cruz Mountains north and northeast of Monterey Bay, and the Diablo and Gabilan ranges inland and to the south, this drainage was cut off. Following these events, tectonic forces raised land inland toward the San Andreas fault zone and northwest towards the Aptos highlands. Between 5 million and 1.8 million years ago, during the Pleistocene epoch, sediments eroded from this uplifted terrain accumulated into geologic formations that were gradually warped downward in the Pajaro Valley. As this depression formed a basin near the shore of what is today Monterey Bay, it was gradually filled with sediments eroded from local marine sandstones and siltstones, along with river-borne sediments from the Pajaro, Salinas, and San Benito river drainages.

During the glacial periods of more recent geologic time, changes in sea level sculpted the six fingers of the sloughs. Rising sea levels filled the slough basin and local river valleys with seawater and fine sediments. When ocean levels fell, the valleys formed by water channels were eroded. Geologists familiar with the area have observed evidence of at least 11 sea-level changes associated with glacial periods in the Aromas Sands, a geologic formation that under-lies the sloughs.

Sea level stood about 100 feet lower than at present during the most recent glacial peri-od, about 18,000 years ago (the late Wisconsinian-Holocene epoch). Locally, the climate was wetter and erosion of the nearby mountains and coastal terraces resulted in the downcutting of streams along roughly the same alignment that we see in the sloughs today. As the climate warmed and the glaciers melted (until about 7,000 years ago), the ocean crept inland, decreas-ing drainage gradients once again. Sediment-filled streams that previously had rushed down steep coastal valleys met rising seas. Sands, silts, clays, and muds slowly settled out of the slackening flows and estuaries that developed in the flat-bottomed backwaters. In the calmest waters, dense blue clays settled out, forming a layer that "perched" the slough water and limited its infiltration into groundwater. Meanwhile, wind and waves worked the local deposits of sand and silt and created coastal dunes. These dunes served as a formidable barrier in the flat topography of the shallow estuary-wetlands complex; as they evolved, they altered the outlets of the Pajaro and Salinas Rivers from time to time.

Throughout the most recent, ongoing period of rising sea level, the coastal landscape has also continued to rise, uplifted by the tectonic forces acting on the Santa Cruz Mountains and the Pajaro Valley. In the Watsonville Sloughs, during periods when coastal uplift has equaled or exceeded sea-level rise, freshwater marshes and deep peat soils have formed. Peat soils evolved over centuries from decaying tules (bulrushes) and other freshwater wetland vegetation up-gradient of the brackish tidewater marshes. These peat soils are found in many reaches of the slough complex, most notably in Struve and Harkins Sloughs. Closer to the ocean, on the floodplain of the Pajaro River, salt and brackish marshes mingled, varying in extent and location with cycles of flooding, sediment deposition, and drought.

In this pattern, over the last 18,000 years, the sloughs have gathered the backwaters of the Pajaro Valley's drainage. They fill when winter rains perch above their impermeable blue clays and saturate the rich organic peats, and they slowly dry out over the summer and fall months each year. The sloughs receive an average of 22 inches of rain annually, generally between November and early May. Most of the water that supports the wetland habitats arrives in this annual flush of rain, via runoff from hill slopes, parking lots, roofs and roads. During the dry periods, a small portion of the water at the surface of the sloughs comes from irrigation runoff and shallow groundwater return flow. Groundwater return flow occurs as rain and irrigation water infiltrate through the uplands and raise the water table above the slough water surface. This groundwater is released to the sloughs as the water table drops to an equilibrium level with adjacent surface water. A small quantity of water from landscape watering also sometimes drains into sections of sloughs near urbanized areas.

Changes to the landscape such as urban development, drainage ditches, road fills, irrigation return flows, and pump systems have altered the timing of water delivery and the quantity and quality of water in the sloughs, yet the lay of the land remains remarkably unchanged. Floodwaters continue to seek the floodplain; our recent impacts have not changed that timeless process.

What we see now, however, is a vestige of the former slough system—the outcome of a fleetingly short (on a geological time scale) chapter on human disturbance and the resilience of a wetland habitat. In 1851, a local farmer, J.B. Hill, used the area's first iron plow to turn soil in the Pajaro Valley. By 1908, drainage projects had installed long, straight ditches that

bisected and dried out the valley's peat-rich bottomlands to open them up to agriculture. For much of this century, farmers carried out intensive dryland cultivation of beans, onions and potatoes on the peat soils of the sloughs. Peat also was mined for fuel. Maps and aerial photographs show that most of the land we now consider wetlands was farmed as recently as the late 1950s and early 1970s. (Different areas went out of production at different times.) And yet, today each of the six major arms of the slough system includes ecologically rich wetland habitat once again.

The regenerative process underway in the Watsonville Slough System is the result of several seemingly disparate factors. First, farming on the formerly seasonally flooded peat bottomland has declined in favor of the cultivation of irrigated row crops on the Pajaro River floodplain, where the protection afforded by flood control levees ensures greater year-round agricultural success. Second, the urbanization of the Watsonville–Buena Vista area has led to the gradual development of residential communities and the elimination of farming in and adjacent to the upper sloughs. Third, the construction of roads, culverts, and roadfills has changed local hydrologic patterns and served to locally back up water in drainage channels, wetland soils, and on former wetland surfaces. Finally, irrigation return flows from berries, lettuce, and row crops now provide a source of surface water in some sections of the sloughs independent of the rainy season.

Considering the long and gradual development of what we now call the Watsonville Sloughs, we can look at its recent history as a lesson on the true scale of geologic time. Despite clearing, draining, paving and other disturbances of the recent past, the slough system demonstrates the resiliency of wetland plant communities. Here, as is seen time and again throughout California, it all comes down to applying the basic recipe for wetlands: Add water, let stand.

—*Gary Kittleson*

Historical and Cultural Setting of the Watsonville Wetlands

Imagine: It is 250 years ago, and you are standing on a small rise under the generous shade of a live oak tree. Below you stretches a maze of tules, water, and bunch grasses. Hundreds of geese, swans, ducks, herons, and other waterbirds crowd the waterway that meanders for miles through the spongy landscape. Their quacks, honks, and whistles greet your ears. A flicker of movement alerts you to a pair of gray foxes passing soundlessly through the foliage to the water's edge. The silvery bodies of steelhead trout glint beneath the water's surface in the midday sun.

Not far inland, the coastal mountains provide a backdrop for the wetlands. The rivers and tributaries that drain the region, as well as the marshes themselves, swell and shrink with the seasons, but food resources—including shellfish, trout, salmon, rabbits, quail, mice, ducks, and bird eggs—are plentiful. Thanks partly to this constant food supply, your village group, the Calendaruc Ohlone, live in relative comfort in what will one day be referred to as the Pajaro ("Bird") Valley.

This image belongs to the past era when the ancestral Ohlone lived their lives in the Pajaro Valley, a basin approximately 10 miles long and 5 to 6 miles wide, situated halfway around the arc of the Monterey Bay. There were between 500 and 900 people in the Pajaro Valley/Castroville area, comprising the largest group around the Monterey Bay. They shifted residences during the year, separating into smaller groups for parts of the year.

The total population of Ohlone peoples in California reached approximately 10,000. In *The Ohlone Way,* Malcolm Margolin describes the coastal terrain between San Francisco Bay and Point Sur, where they dwelled, prior to European arrival: "Water was virtually everywhere, especially where the land was flat. Places that are now dry were then described as having springs, brooks, ponds—even fairly large lakes. In the days before channelizations, all the major rivers—the Carmel, Salinas, Pajaro, Coyote Creek, and Alameda Creek—as well as many minor streams, spread out each winter and spring to form wide, marshy valleys."

For centuries, perhaps millennia, the Pajaro Valley environment supported a broad diversity of life. Grizzly bears, beavers, elk, deer, raptors, songbirds, foxes, raccoons, turtles, snakes, fishes, insects, and humans coexisted in its varied and plentiful habitats. The richest of these habitats were the wetlands, made up of six interconnected sloughs today called Struve, West Branch Struve, Harkins, Hanson, and Gallighan, all of which ultimately flowed into Watsonville Slough. This slough system, along with the lakes and the Pajaro River, was the dominant natural feature of Pajaro Valley.

Despite sweeping alterations from agriculture, housing, and industry over the last two and a half centuries, the wetlands, like a giant heart, now still pulse with life. They circulate, filter, and recharge the water they receive, and they nurture a complex web of plant and animal life. They are the home of a variety of rare, threatened, and endangered species, including 27 of the 73 at-risk birds listed in California as "Species of Special Concern."

This book is about preserving that heartbeat. The efforts to do so require an understanding of the changing relationships between humans and the land, as the region's history bears out. Humans have ushered in three major waves of transformation to the wetlands, resculpting the land and culture on a vast scale.

THE OHLONE TIME

From excavations of shell mounds and kitchen middens, we know the Calendaruc and other Ohlone tribes followed the gathering and hunting traditions of their ancestors. They collected mussels, clams, and other shellfish from the coastal zone; trapped fish and birds; and hunted sea otters and sea lions from rafts constructed of reeds. Whales and other marine mammals that occasionally beached or washed up dead on the bay shores provided scavenging opportunities, though the people had to keep a careful watch for numerous grizzly bears who also were attracted to this food resource. From inland areas the Ohlones also gathered such fruits of the forests as acorns, buckeyes, and various seeds, as well as plant fiber, for use in crafting dwellings and baskets. These early dwellers of the Pajaro Valley also hunted large mammals such as deer and elk.

With a diet that drew from a range of biotic communities, the impacts of the area's indigenous people were spread among many plant and animal species without appreciably diminishing the numbers of any particular group. Moreover, they lived with a sense of close connection to the world around them. As Margolin writes: "Their intimate knowledge of animals did not lead to conquest, nor did their familiarity breed contempt. The Ohlones lived in a world where people were few and animals were many, where the bow and arrow were the height of technology, where a deer who was not approached in the proper manner could easily escape, and a bear might conceivably attack—indeed, they lived in a world where the animal kingdom had not yet fallen under the domination of the human race and where people did not yet see themselves as the undisputed lords of all creation."

With food and materials for tools so readily available, the Ohlones had no need to develop agriculture, but they left their mark on the land in another very significant way. By setting fire to the land after harvesting seeds in autumn they discouraged the growth of large woody plants and promoted the regrowth of the perennial grasses and other plants they used. By transporting seeds, they spread plant and tree species to new locations. These practices altered

the balance of vegetation types and the animals associated with them. The basic element of their approach to the land was to take only what was needed. In sum, the values and life-style of the region's Native Americans were very different from those of the European and American settlers to come.

THE SPANISH-MEXICAN PERIOD

In 1769 Captain Gaspar de Portola, Governor of Baja California, led an expedition of 64 men up the coast of what is now the state of California. They arrived in the Pajaro Valley in October. The diaries of Miguel Costanso and Father Juan Crespi, members of the expedition, tell of the rich and vibrant plain they found, with lakes, streams, rolling hills and abundant wildlife. According to the diaries, the people of the area were quite startled by the sight of men on horseback, but friendly nonetheless. Portola's group camped on the bank of the river discovered by his scouts, not far from a village bordered by lush bottomland. Here they found cottonwoods, sycamores, live oaks, and another tree they had never seen before, which they called palo colorado, or red timber. This was the first recorded European sighting of the California redwood, *Sequoia sempervirens.*

When Portola and his men returned to the village that their scouts had visited days earlier, they found it abandoned, but among the items left behind were the bodies of a large bird stuffed with grass, and half the body of a black bird suspended from a pole. Both sightings have been speculated as the origin for the name, El Rio del Pajaro, or Bird River.

The dense vegetation in and around the valley made travel difficult for Portola's party, so they took a northerly course. Many were sick with scurvy and diarrhea. The group rested for four days in the vicinity of College Lake (the Spanish name was Laguna Grande), near what is today Casserly Road. In all, this first visit of the Spaniards to the Pajaro Valley totaled only eight days, but it ushered in an era of radical changes to the area.

Not long after Portola's expedition, the Spanish began to settle in the valley. Their numbers were small, but their collective footprint transformed the area in irreversible ways, taking a heavy toll on native peoples as well as plant and animal species. The Calendaruc and other Ohlone tribes were decimated, victims of European diseases and mistreatment and the loss of their land and culture. According to reports of the era, as late as 1847 the Pajaro Valley supported a sparse population of about 40 Spaniards and a few remaining native people while serving as a vast, unfenced pasture ground for their herds of cattle, sheep, and horses.

In contrast to the age of agricultural development that followed, the Spanish concentrated their energies on ranching. They (and later the Americans) used fire on a greater scale than the Ohlone to clear land for cattle grazing. This heavy disturbance of the land and the many exotic plants introduced in association with the cattle industry—including the wild oat, filaree, mustard, wild radish, foxtail and bur clover still prominent in the valley—displaced most of the native plants. The Spanish system of land grants, called ranchos, left another legacy that has survived into the present day: the former rancho boundaries provided much of the framework for subdivisions around the Pajaro Valley and other parts of the Monterey Bay region. Many of the names of these ranchos are familiar to area residents today, including Rancho Los Corralitos, Rancho Salsipuedes, Rancho San Andreas, Rancho la Laguna de las Calabazas, and Rancho Bolsa del Pajaro.

So great was the transformation of the environment of the Pajaro Valley between Portola's arrival in 1769 and the incorporation of Watsonville in 1868, it has sometimes been compared to the transition in Europe from a hunting and gathering economy to an agricultural one—which took centuries to accomplish. In fact, the changes witnessed in the Pajaro Valley during a mere 100-year period were only a prelude of what was to come.

THE AMERICAN ERA

⟶

American settlers streaming into the Pajaro Valley after the California Gold Rush of 1848 in many ways accelerated the trends of change to the environment. They introduced many more exotic plant species, which today number in the hundreds. Those who are familiar with the valley's river and stream corridors know the prevalence of German ivy and periwinkle, two very invasive non-native plants. Throughout the valley, logging, land clearing and drainage activities, and urban construction further reduced the ranges of the native plants and created conditions suitable for other invasive non-natives, such as poison hemlock and European grasses, to thrive. The outcome has been that many native plant varieties have disappeared and many others are seriously threatened or close to extinction. This reduces the food sources for many native insects, birds, and animals.

Impacts on animal life have been dramatic. Early on, grizzly bears, tule elk, and other animals valuable to hunters or considered threats were wiped out, while marine species such as the California sea otter and humpback and gray whales were hunted nearly to extinction in Monterey Bay. On the other hand, populations of certain animals considered pests, such as the ground squirrel, exploded, in part due to the loss of their predators and other ecological changes.

During the latter half of the 1800s, commercial agriculture took off in the Pajaro Valley. Draining, dredging, grading, filling and the channeling of waterways were carried out on a massive scale to make large tracts of land suitable for agriculture. William H. Brewer, a member of the Whitney expedition commissioned to produce a Geological Survey of California, described in one of his letters the character of agriculture in the valley on August 2, 1861. "On the river is Watsonville, a neat, thriving, bustling, American-looking little town. The country around is in the very highest cultivation, divided into farms, covered with the heaviest of grain, or a still heavier crop of weeds. Several threshing machines were seen in the fields. . . ." Farming in the Pajaro Valley flourished, transitioning from wheat to a succession of crops including sugar beets, fruit (especially apple) orchards, row crops, and berries.

After the American settlers, Chinese, Japanese, German, Slavonian, Filipino, Portuguese and other groups of immigrants to the valley shaped the intensive wave of agricultural development that took place as the century closed.

To move this bounty around California and beyond, roadways, railroads and a shipping dock at Palm Beach were constructed, further changing the landscape. This was followed by new businesses, especially agriculturally related enterprises, and housing for those who worked in these and other jobs. The cumulative impacts of these activities on the Pajaro Valley wetlands continue today, and they are a theme in many of the essays that follow in this book.

WHAT LIES AHEAD FOR THE PAJARO VALLEY?

At the close of the 1990s, the 800-plus farms in the Pajaro Valley brought in more than $750 million, making the region one of the top-ranking agricultural production areas in the world. Without the unique and rich combination of natural resources here—particularly the climate, water, and soil as well as workers who plant, harvest, and transport the crops—such wealth would not be possible.

At the start of the new millennium, the strongest pressures acting on the valley's environment are related to the urban expansion that is rapidly transforming the area. Demand for housing for the labor force of job-rich Silicon Valley, as well as unprecedented real estate speculation and a booming economy, have made the Pajaro Valley a prime target for increased urban development.

While increased urbanization generally results in the loss of farmlands, in the case of the Pajaro Valley, wetland and upland habitats are also at risk. Close to 85 percent of the valley's former wetlands have already succumbed to development and transformation of the land, resulting in loss of both numbers and diversity of plant and animal species. But other ecological threats remain. These include continuing effects of numerous domesticated animals as well as plant and insect pests that alter the ecological balance. Changes in agricultural practices have created a groundwater overdraft, resulting in the intrusion of seawater into regional aquifers. Heavy usage of agricultural chemicals pollutes soil, water and air, affecting humans and ecosystems as a whole.

Despite damage to its ecological functions, the Watsonville Slough System is still a rich natural resource. With restoration, it has the potential to regain some of what has been lost. What lies ahead for Pajaro Valley's disappearing natural resources, including its unique wetlands, will constitute a fourth wave of transformation in the cultural and natural record of the area. As students, parents, workers and residents, we will make critical choices that will affect the future environment of the Pajaro Valley region.

We can take the path of continuing to devastate the wetlands and their plants and animals with shopping centers and housing tracts. Or we can take the more difficult road of finding ways to provide housing that is truly affordable to those who live and work in the Pajaro Valley, along with jobs that pay a living wage, while still preserving the wetlands for the future.

We can be a model for the rest of the country and for future generations. Or we can be yet another example of a place where the richness of the wetlands will just be part of the story told in history books of what life was like, once upon a time, not so long ago.

—*Christine Johnson-Lyons*

REFERENCES

Margolin, Malcom. *The Ohlone Way.* Heyday Press, Berkeley, CA 1978 (2nd edition).

Gordon, Burton L. *Monterey Bay Area: Natural History and Cultural Imprints.* Boxwood Press, Pacific Grove, CA 1996 (3rd edition).

Brewer, William H. *Up and Down California.* University of California Press, Berkeley, CA. 1974.

Slough Niches

by Jerry Busch

MAP OF HARKINS SLOUGH

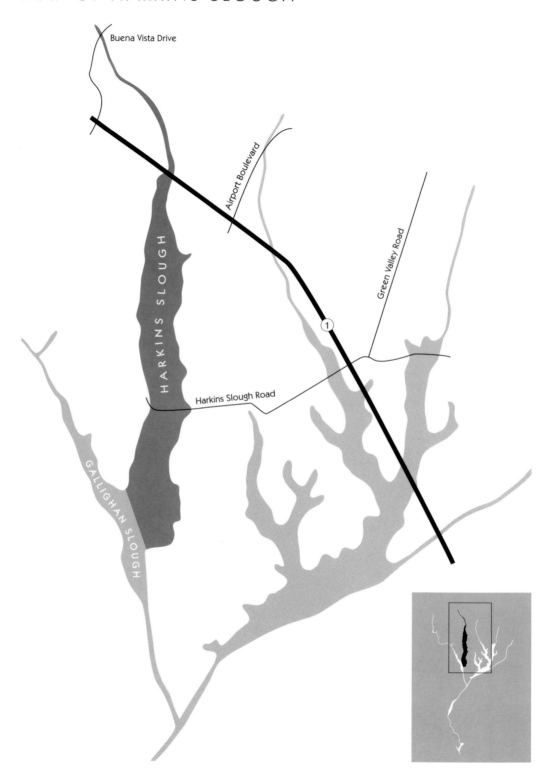

Buena Vista Drive

Airport Boulevard

Green Valley Road

HARKINS SLOUGH

Harkins Slough Road

GALLIGHAN SLOUGH

1

Harkins Slough

Harkins Slough is the largest and most north-reaching slough in the Watsonville system. It receives drainage from Larkin Valley and flows westward under Highway One, between Buena Vista Road and Airport Boulevard. Here it broadens, often flooding Harkins Slough Road. Gallighan Slough, which is inaccessible, merges into Harkins Slough at a point below the county landfill. Harkins Slough continues south and joins Watsonville Slough east of San Andreas Road. It can be viewed from Harkins Slough Road west of Highway One.

SNAPSHOTS OF A SLOUGH

Sitting home, miles from the slough and separated from it by walls and windows, you can forget just how alive and enduring Watsonville's wetlands are. The mutilated slough with its torn-up hillsides, its bent stems, its winter flocks gone, seems unappealing. But you rise to go forth for another look. It is this series of "snapshots"—a kind of picture album—which informs your work.

At nine o'clock on a March morning, Harkins Slough is in an uproar. Song sparrows serenade tirelessly. The coots sound like the soundtrack of a Tarzan movie. A restless kite glides by, whistling noisily. Crows caw at every excuse, making a complex variety of vocalizations, all seeming to communicate annoyance. A woodpecker drums. Most mysterious, and touching, is the pump of a bittern, a rare sound indeed. There are no "conk-a-ree" calls from red-winged blackbirds, however; their habitat here has been ploughed. Overhead, violet-green and tree swallows twitter softly.

Egrets fleck the slough with white. The water level has fallen enough that they are concentrated along the ditch and in a pocket by the willows. Some, sated from fishing, stand idly among the clumps of dried cattails. A moorhen dabbles delicately about, its crimson beak flashing. A few cinnamon teal ducks also dabble nearby. After a while they haul out and stand awkwardly on willow limbs, as if disgusted by the green slime in the shallows here.

A gorgeous red-shouldered hawk flies, screaming, into a tall chartreuse willow. A Cooper's hawk exits the willow, then disappears into the leafless hollow of a dead oak. The kite glides by again, calling, and lands near the red-shouldered. He has a deer mouse in his talons. A red-tailed hawk swoops by, fast and low. The red-shouldered darts off, and the kite relocates out into the slough.

I see the bittern standing in the open marsh, beak upraised. Its beak jerks down and a pouch-like apparatus in its throat begins to rise and fall. After a moment I hear the pumping sound wafting over the reeds. The bird's movement looks like hard work. It rests. A pair of crows lands in the green, slimy muck. The stuff is so dense they can almost walk on it, yet many grebes, teals, herons, and other birds forage in and around it.

Trios of mallards and teals zoom around, tracing filigree designs in the slough air as they pair up. Cormorants, their fishing done, glide in desultory flights up the slough, then down, looking prehistoric. The egrets vie over puddles, and two tree swallows battle, tumbling through the sky. A loud squawking announces the return of the red-shouldered hawk, this time chased by a red-tailed cousin. Before the red-shouldered is halfway across the slough, another red-tailed swoops wickedly at him, missing narrowly. Meanwhile, the Cooper's hawk in the oak has disappeared.

I am always amazed by the slough's vitality. An abundance of animals is always here, struggling for food, territory, and mates—in short, survival. The slough could flourish if only the grassland, coastal scrub, and forest habitats that help support it were enabled to regenerate into more healthy states. There is a nucleus of life here to be saved.

A WING AND A PRAYER

There was a time when hardly a single white-tailed kite could be found in California, the only state in the union where this bird ranges, outside a small area in Texas.

I grew up in country well suited for kites—the live-oak savanna of central San Benito County—without seeing one until I was maybe ten years old. It was in the very field where my playmates and I flew paper kites that I saw my first bird kite. It hovered and scalloped about, thrilling me as it fell upon its prey like an angel of death.

We were experiencing a rodent population explosion that had occurred that year. Any stone or old wood you overturned revealed a vole, mouse, or nest. Voles are lemming relatives and, like them, are bulky and blunt-nosed. In the northern tundra, lemming populations become so dense they are forced to move in thick marches, attracting great gray, snowy, and hawk owls, packs of foxes and wolves, and every other predator in the territory. In California, kites, short-eared owls, marsh hawks, and other raptors behave similarly. Particularly in winter when food is short, they rove widely, searching out the places where voles and mice have become populous. Such behavior helped the kites to rapidly recolonize past territories as its population rebounded from its low ebb in the '50s and '60s.

During the kites' darkest years when DDT usage was ravaging raptor populations, kites never left off breeding in Harkins Slough. Though the Pajaro Valley used plenty of DDT, the slough watersheds, impacted mostly by dairy operations, had lower concentrations of the insecticide so deadly to birds. Abundant populations of voles and invertebrates at the slough kept resident pairs of kites on site year-round. From scattered enclaves such as this, the species bounced back wondrously.

But the slough's resident kites, which have bred here for a very long time, now face a new threat: development that would pave over the prey-rich hillside vole towns and bring in more house cats likely to polish off any survivors. One by one, as the hillsides of Watsonville's urban sloughs have succumbed to development, their resident kites have vanished.

And as the kites go, so go the other raptors. In years when rodent populations swell, 20 or more species head in droves to the terrace lands west of Watsonville to join in the feast. Many of these, including great-horned owls, and kestrels, red-shouldered and red-tailed hawks, breed there, as do the kites.

The angel-like stoop of the kite, wherein it poises its wings straight over its back and drops lightly to the ground, is one of the great sights of nature. No less so is the courtship flight, in which the amorous kite couple locks talons and helicopters earthward, upside-down, breaking apart only a few feet from the ground. My prayer is simple. Let them stay.

WATCHING THE WEST SIDE

Watching, I am watched. Great blue herons, three in succession, arrive on the wide, shallow pond in upper Harkins Slough and fix their piercing glares on me as I focus my binoculars on them. The withdrawal of my notebook from my pack gives pause to several gadwalls, and a Beechy ground squirrel whistles alarm.

Feigning disinterest, I focus on my lunch. Crows, watching and cawing from hidden vantage points, are not disarmed. Meanwhile, the graceful, debonair black-necked stilts are absorbed in their own pursuits and pay me no attention. Killdeers cry shrilly in conversation with each other. Two of them dance in a circle, their ruddy tails flashing. Among the shorebirds, only a solitary alert yellowlegs seems aware of my hunkered-down form near the toe of a slope shaded by oaks.

The striking black-and-white plumage of avocets attracts my attention. Sixteen of them feed in a phalanx across the pond in one to three inches of water. Their heads veer from side to side as, beaks ajar, they literally rake the mud's surface for invertebrates. Their legs follow their heads in a kind of drunken, delayed motion. After an hour of this mud-searching, half of them pause for awhile to preen, then resume formation.

While the avocets sweep, the long-billed dowitchers perforate the mud. A flock of more than 200, sectioned into groups of a several dozen, probe incessantly. They methodically cover all the unflooded surfaces—perhaps 15 percent of the open area. Shoulder-high stalks of smartweed arch over the surrounding peat. The generous number of birds currently here (at least 450) is a reflection of this half-acre pond's "well-stocked larder." In the weeks to come

the smartweeds' long, nodding flower-heads will produce a huge bounty of seeds favored by migrating songbirds and water birds, some of which will spend the winter here.

I take note of the pond's other beneficiaries. Three semipalmated plovers and a Bonaparte's gull are picking about the shore, while a dozen or so phalaropes poke around the water. A green-winged teal paddles in the shallows with 25 mallards. A great egret, three marbled godwits, and flocks of Western sandpipers are visible on the muddy shoreline.

Would development on the east hillside of upper Harkins Slough adversely affect this life? I think so. It would seem that the hillside's numerous seeps, slumps, draws, and relatively steep slopes should serve to rebuff development. And yet these features of the terrain are no more extreme than at the edges of East Struve, where development has more or less endured—to that slough's detriment. Will it be any different here?

MAP OF HANSON SLOUGH

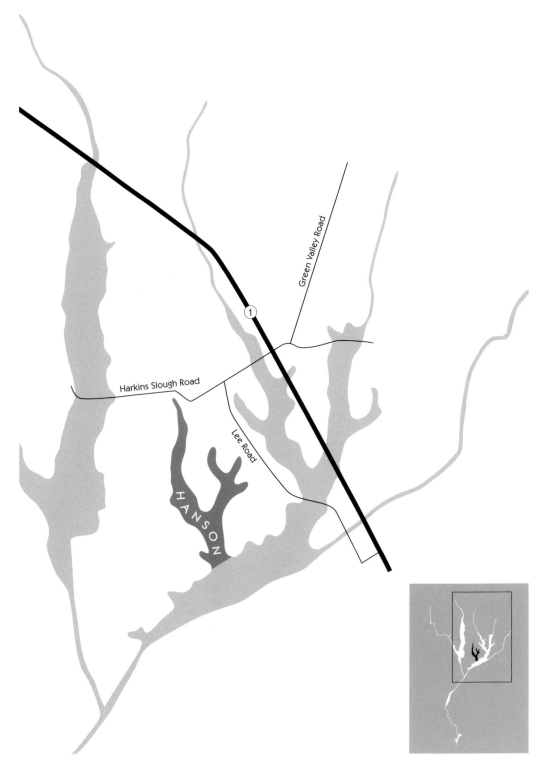

Green Valley Road

Harkins Slough Road

Lee Road

H A N S O N

Hanson Slough

Hanson Slough is located west of High-way One and Lee Road. Its upper reaches can be seen from Harkins Slough Road. West of Lee Road it feeds into Watsonville Slough midway between Highway One and San Andreas Road. Unfortunately, it is not readily accessible to the public, although aquisition efforts are underway.

GREBELAND

There is nothing like a little water to improve a wetland, and the heavy rains of the late 1990s have brought water by the bucketful to the freshwater sloughs of the Pajaro Valley. The spring rain that slaps across car windshields, blurring the images of raptors hunched on tree branches and posts as we pass the sloughs, also streams over the Purisima rock outcroppings in Aptos, the sand hills edged by Freedom Boulevard, and the wide Pajaro Valley floor. Eventually this water runs into the great peat sponge of the sloughs.

On this day in lower Hanson Slough, the pools are home to hungry pied-billed grebe babies. You can tell they are hungry because they peep when they want to eat. Industriously the mother grebes seek to blunt their offsprings' growing appetites. They dive for crawdads, periodically hooting very loudly and rapidly: "HOO-WOO-Woo-wo-wo-wo-wo!" Having no teeth, the babies gulp the crawdads whole. Their eyes open wide when they are presented with one of these delicacies; without ceremony, they grab it greedily and speed off to swallow it as rapidly as possible.

Although crawdads possess pincers and menacing claws that spread wide (and a bad attitude), this doesn't seem to deter the baby grebes in the slightest. They turn the crawdad head-first and proceed to gulp it down as a viper might do. After a spasm or two along the grebe's gullet, the previously formidable crustacean is reduced to a lump above the gizzard. Then it is past the gizzard, and the baby grebe is ready to do it all again.

It happens that in this part of the slough there's a lovely patch of tules, an ideal spot where the zebra-faced grebe youngsters can hide quietly, until mother delivers the next treat. It's nothing less than a tule pied-billed grebe preschool.

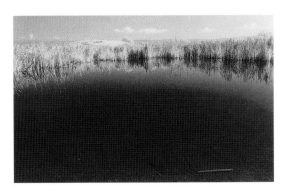

Grebes are considered "low" birds on the evolutionary ladder because their bone structure and other physical attributes indicate they are products of an earlier phase of evolution than many birds. Grebe fossils, which include some of the oldest in the avian kingdom, show little change over many millennia. Grebe feet are lobed, rather than webbed, yet those clunky lobed feet do the job: the duck hasn't drawn a breath that can outswim the grebe or so efficiently capture elusive swimming prey under the dark duckweed mats. Ancient, yes, but slow, never.

A TREE SWALLOW SINGS

West of the heaps of apple-wood ash smoldering along Lee Road, past the "chivos y puercos" sign of Lee-Harkins Farm, lies the verdant expanse of Hanson Slough. It is the most secluded, least monitored, and arguably most beautiful of the three sloughs west of Highway One.

Amid the cacophony of an April morning at the slough, a male tree swallow sings in a willow near the ponds, exercising a voice as diminutive as the feet that tether it to its twig. The bird takes off from its perch and scours the air for insects, occasionally swirling after them like a turbo-powered flycatcher, its metallic-green plumage flashing.

A bit deeper in the wood is an old willow snag, broken off by a recent windstorm, perhaps 20 feet above the ground. The broad stump of the main trunk is visible through foliage. I can see a woodpecker hole in the section left standing, and from it—aahaa!—peers the delicate head of the singing swallow's mate.

The spacious "condo" where she rests is easily large enough to accommodate a European starling, and this could mean trouble. Tree swallows and their violet-green swallow cousins have held their ground against the aggressive starlings better than bluebirds and others, partly because swallows are small enough to occupy holes inaccessible to starlings. But this cavity, recently rendered more visible due to windstorm damage, has the potential for becoming a setting for eviction proceedings.

The male is taking a few turns through the air, staying within a radius of about 40 yards from the nest tree. He alights on his perch momentarily, and then glides down to hang from the lip of the cavity by his little toes, propping against his tail feathers like a woodpecker. He peers in.

Suddenly the male is in the air again, hotly pursued by a rival. The two zoom through the branches at breakneck speed, the intruder zeroing in with dive-bomb attacks and the retreating male responding with evasive maneuvers. After several moments of this seemingly ineffectual defense, the interloper withdraws. The skirmish demonstrates that nesting cavities are in high demand.

Now, a new surprise: Another tree swallow flies by the nest cavity. Its metallic-brown wings quiver downward in a display that suggests it is a juvenile. It makes a couple of passes, low and slow, before exiting. Tree swallows are renowned philanderers; something like a third of all their offspring are fathered by males other than the females' "official" mates. Is this bird a straying female trying to "get into the genes" of a successful property-owner? The cavity-sitting female eyes her mate, while he perches primly, seeming to affect disinterest. After these disturbances, the pair collects themselves together for a few minutes near his favored perch. Then he's off again, and shortly she is, too.

By mid-morning the sun is hot, and save for the persevering efforts of song sparrows and Wilson's warblers, the wood has grown quiet. At intervals, a flock of 16 or so tree swallows dances by, probably still on migration. Often one or both of the pair rise to join them. But they never stray far from their nest site, and they check the cavity frequently. Occasionally they fly in tandem and sing to each other in the air.

MARSH MANEUVERS

A glowering January sky darkens Hanson Slough. The willow copse below the barnyard is silent and motionless, its only apparent occupants a pair of hairy woodpeckers pecking at scattered targets. Broken boughs gleam through wind-raked foliage.

I edge along the weedy tracks between the willow copse and the fava bean fields grateful that the barnyard dog—a grim mix of Australian shepherd and mastiff—has ceased its harangue.

At the pool where the farm property meets the slough floor, I interrupt the breakfast of a pair of gadwalls, and they melt into the reeds. I freeze and wait, screened by willow shoots.

I have parked near a virtual gallery of teal ducks. As I watch, pairs and individuals emerge from the top of a lane that extends down the slough between clumps of cattails. The ducks convene beneath the black branches of a lone willow. I admire the males, resplendent in a mixture of creamy hues, grays, cinnamon, and a shade of forest green that would make Eddie Bauer weep with envy.

Posture erect and not a feather out of place, a pair of drakes cruises up, looking for action. The muted light hints at iridescence in their headgear. Eventually, about eight males puff up and turn in tight, ceremonial circles, ebony and gold flashing beneath their upraised tails. A female watches attentively, though she seems to be "spoken for" by the handsomest of the group.

Another male—this one with less than impeccable grooming—announces his entry, as all the previous ones have done, with a reedy whistle from the top of the lane. A pair of males responds with hostility, inflating their chests like drill recruits. The would-be joiner of the group acquiesces by turning aside and preening deferentially.

Up the lane strolls a sedate pair, male and female. The female's entrance elicits a chorus of whistles, which she acknowledges with an affable head bob and husky quack. This pair shortly departs, leaving perhaps a dozen males vying for the single hen in their company.

At 10:15 the sun breaks out and beams warmly through a break in the procession of over-sized, gray clouds, signaling the transition to midday. The light elicits a surge in slough noises. A thrush chirps, dueling tree frogs creak, a warbler twits, a phoebe calls, a mallard honks, coots hoot. Song sparrows, occupying exposed perches, sing loudly, while a wren scolds. On the crest of the hill down-slough, a flicker careens to a high perch, rufous wings flashing. It peruses the desolate farm fields adjacent to the slough. No ants there. The bird flies off along the edge of the marsh to cloistering hill slopes.

I move to leave, again disrupting the unfortunate gadwalls, which had, after more than an hour's wait, just resumed their meal. I stop at the mouth of Hanson Slough, where it joins Watsonville Slough. I gaze out at a thousand waterfowl floating over thinly flooded farm fields dotted with cocklebur stalks. Four snow geese graze on new lettuce across the way. About 70 canvasbacks stop diving and move in the opposite direction from me—out of shotgun range? A flock of perhaps a hundred ring-necked ducks skitters airborne, circles a few times, passes over the Harkins Slough peat ponds, then resettles. Unlike mallards and other "tipping" ducks that favor the protective cover of willows, ring-necks, canvasbacks, and other diving ducks occupy clear runways of open water.

I depart, leaving over a thousand waterfowl undisturbed.

MAP OF STRUVE SLOUGH

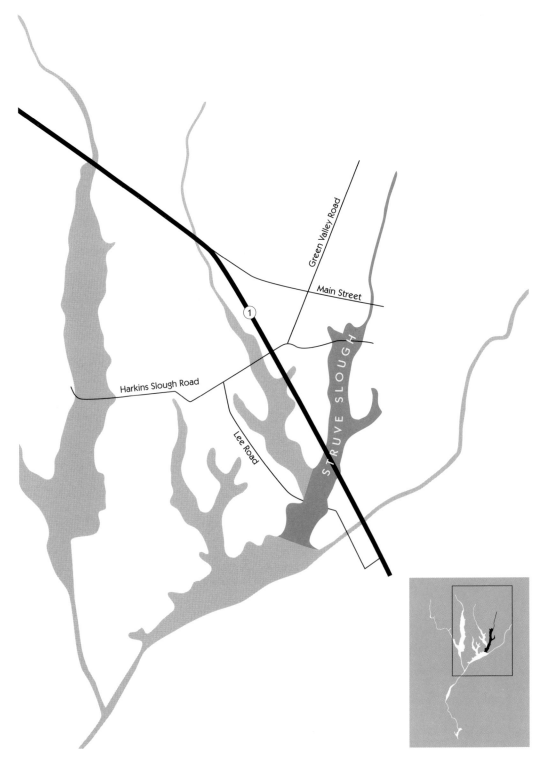

Struve Slough

Struve Slough begins near Pennsylvania Avenue and Green Valley Road, draining behind Watsonville Square Shopping Center and crossing under Main Street, Harkins Slough Road, and Highway One before joining West Struve Slough between Highway One and Lee Road. Struve Slough often floods Lee Road. It can be viewed from any of these roads. The City of Watsonville is planning to install a slough-side walking path.

A DAY IN THE LIFE

Ever see a duck get up in the morning? Ducks' eyes are bright when they rise, as are ours in the wild. The fuchsia sunlight over Struve Slough on this dawning January morning finds most of the waterbirds asleep. A great egret standing close to the industrial park is dozing, head hunched on its shoulders, long neck folded, waiting for sufficient light—and motivation—to find a frog or fish for breakfast. A kingfisher atop a willow is motionless, in stark contrast with its energetic darting during the day. Among the mallards, shovelers, gadwalls and coots on the slough, only the coots are active, poking about the water surface. The ducks bob silently, heads tucked in wings. One duck—the designated watchbird—seems to be on lookout. Yet even he shows no concern about the man with binoculars in a truck across the way. Like most birds, waterfowl get used to seeing cars everywhere and will often let them get closer than a person on foot.

After a while a large mallard drake lifts his head, stretches out his neck, and beats his wings, half lifting himself out of the water. He looks around. A female and several males floating near him have their heads out now, too. The drake swims up behind the female, neck arched, beak tucked, the feathers on his head and neck puffed out. The female swims along gently, and he follows her closely for a few moments, reasserting their pair bond. The big drake veers toward a smaller drake nearby. The smaller one gives way, recognizing the larger bird's dominance.

In a few moments the ducks gather in a small area of open water. All the drakes are posturing, but the big one stays closer to the female than the others. Nearby, a green-winged teal drake is displaying to a hen, bobbing his beak up and down. During their courtship, she will respond in kind. Meanwhile, a shoveler duck loiters very close by, watching attentively.

The day's social order restated, the mallards bathe and preen, sloshing water over their backs and wings. Daily ablutions maintain a clean, light film of oil on the surface of their feathers that keeps the plumage water-tight and the down beneath it dry and warm. Finally, the birds start breakfast, dabbling about on the water surface for seeds that have dropped from surrounding dock, bulrushes and sedges. A few mallards fly in from elsewhere, each tasting the slough water upon landing.

It is known that many geese mate for life. On the other hand, ducks are believed to mate for only a season at a time, but their pair bonds are strong. Later this day I see a hunter kill a beautiful little female hooded merganser as she flies by his illegal blind in Harkins Slough. When she tumbles into the water, her mate circles back and hovers about, searching for her despite the danger, departing only when grazed himself by buckshot.

(Author's note: In 1999, four years after this was written, the wetlands and an upland parcel next to this site in Harkins Slough were purchased by the Open Space Alliance of Santa Cruz County in a transaction precipitated by Watsonville Wetlands Watch.)

BOUQUETS-A-BUZZ

A rampaging herd of bulldozers, scrapers, and loaders is rearranging the hillside ecology alongside Struve Slough at North Main Street in Watsonville. My favorite incipient slough, a deep swale carved by centuries of seeping water, is being transformed into a pile of dirt. Dust rises and drifts back toward the city. At the orange cordon demarcating the destruction zone, a displaced family of mockingbirds flaps restlessly back and forth, quarreling over perches in remnant patches of fennel and blackberries. A singing Anna's hummingbird also numbers among the refugees, the bird's lovely creaking song still bubbling irrepressibly out of its neon throat.

I recall a winter's day about a decade ago, when the west bank of the slough was home to a colony of ground squirrels and affiliated burrowing owls. The thundering herd in the swale then was only a small group of domesticated buffaloes. Down in the sopping muck where the swale fed the slough, a hundred or so common snipe, usually a solitary species, gobbled up the worms that had proliferated in soils nourished by buffalo pies.

I've been told that beneath this bog the carcass of a farmer's tractor decays—a reminder of the patient and blessed appetite of the unconquerable muck for all things leaden. If the hillside seeps are a hindrance, the slough floors are all but unconquerable. The tractor's grave on this September morning is honored by a floral display that would embarrass royalty. In the slough's center, an elliptical patch of bur marigold blooms in Van Goghesque sprays of yellows. Surrounding it is a glorious horseshoe of fat hen, its purple tips aglow with late summer blush. Dashes of pink and rose from half a dozen varieties of smartweed round out the bouquet.

The bugs are beside themselves. By fall, second and third generations of the year are reproducing, and the slough serves as their all-in-one restaurant, bar, and bedroom, buzzing with a billion buggy schemes. I dive into the fat hen, almost colliding with a great armor-suited stinkbug. Just a juvenile, it is outrageously bedecked in green triangular shields with an abdomen protected by a bright hardened integument that looks like russet chain-mail with rows of cream-colored rivets. The husky insect clambers slowly through the tall foliage, pausing to scrape off its rapier-like mouth parts before moving off.

Tiny, metallic-orange hover flies vibrate musically in the breezeways. A pair of cabbage white butterflies, as if united by an invisible cord, skitters through the air at a frenetic pace. Dragonflies course above the field at low angles like marsh harriers, their flights interwoven with—and occasionally intersecting —those of skippers, wasps, bees, and leafhoppers. A fly pauses on a bur marigold bloom to suck up nectar, its impossibly plump striped rear end looking more honey-filled than the bees it mimics.

As I lie on my stomach, lost in this miniature world, my heart skips a beat when an enormous black, furry caterpillar, representing some species of moth, trundles over my leg. Nearby on a smartweed flower, a pair of copulating painted-lady butterflies attracts attention. After perhaps 45 minutes of connubial stillness, the female half of the bow-tied couple rouses and begins trying, unsuccessfully, to shove off the male.

Downstream, across Harkins Slough Road, I wander into a patch of showy pink lady's thumb flower, which has slowly expanded over the years from a triangle shape into a diamond. The blooming smartweeds are ripe with seed that showers down, rattling on dead cattail stalks as I pass. Flocks of seed-eating house finches and goldfinches flit to and from willows, and everywhere song sparrows flutter up like grasshoppers. A shrike sits in the alcove of a willow island surrounded by a sea of bur marigolds. Against the backdrop of taller willows and cattails in the distance, the scene looks like the setting of an Audubon painting. I glance away for a moment and the shrike vanishes.

Up on a terrace across from West Marine, I flush a pair of doves from the underbrush. A merlin rockets over my right shoulder and skims out of sight over hemlock tops, rises back into view, and jets off. Merlins seem to have but one forward speed: flat out. The velocity and trajectory of its flight is the merlin's single identifying characteristic: all other field marks necessarily blur.

My visit to this realm beyond the North Main Street devastation leaves me with one consoling thought: There is still a lot of life here on these urban terrace-sides not yet laid waste by the intractable bulldozers.

GOING, GOING, GONE!

One by one, as the human population grows, the diversity of species with which we share the planet shrinks. Humans not only take up space physically, we also damage ecosystems by disrupting habitats, eliminating key predators, introducing exotic species and polluting land and water. We see this happening now in the slough lands west of Watsonville where wildlife is indeed disappearing.

A striking example of this is the burrowing owl, known to old-time ranchers as the "billy owl." It was one of the first birds to vanish from the sloughs, gradually dwindling and disappearing as, one by one, the slough's dairy farms—Hanson, Struve, Harkins, Cardoza—were sold and their herds taken away. Without cattle to keep the grass grazed short, ground squirrels couldn't see their predators; without the ground squirrels the burrowing owls lost their food source and their burrow makers. They, too, left.

No longer does this unique raptor pop out of the ground at your feet, flying off with buoyant strokes to settle on a fence post and glare fiercely about, occasionally indulging in a quick knee bend. Now all but extirpated from Santa Cruz County, burrowing owls underscore the fragility of many ecological relationships: remove one seemingly unrelated element, like grazing, and the ecosystem fails.

Ground-nesting birds are generally among the first to be eliminated when wetland ecosystems are disturbed. Foxes, weasels, skunks, raccoons, and domesticated predators such as cats and dogs, introduced by humans, find these birds easy prey. The short-eared owl is still sometimes seen, but it is rare and also in jeopardy. Short-eared owls nest in the tall grass of marshlands and work the evening swing shift, flying along aerial courses patrolled during the day by marsh harriers, another ground-nester that no longer breeds in the sloughs. Though not closely related, these two raptors arrived at similar hunting styles through eons of mutual gliding over expanses of grasses that offered no perches. Nowadays, with each acre of grassland claimed by "progress," another segment of the grassland raptor population disappears.

Virginia rails and soras, two other ground-nesters vulnerable to wetland habitat loss and to predation, are quail-sized birds that dodge quietly through the fens searching for small prey. These species are scarce and threatened in the sloughs. The two other varieties of rail—the clapper rail and the sparrow-sized black rail—are on the endangered list in California.

Wildlife species that form colonies are also highly vulnerable to human interruption. Night herons, which had apparently established a breeding colony in Hanson Slough, have not been seen there in recent years. Tricolored blackbirds, candidates for state endangered status, until recently maintained a thriving colony in Hanson Slough, one of the few left in the county. Now they, too, are gone.

Bank swallow colonies that once graced the slough disappeared years ago. In past years we have also lost yellow-billed cuckoos, yellow-breasted chats and Bell's vireos. Watsonville Slough's red-legged frog population was for years thought to be limited to one small pond near Harkins Slough. There they were out of reach of the fiercely predatory introduced bull-frog, which has all but killed off the resident pond turtles.

The effects of increasing human populations on the numbers and diversity of wildlife are sometimes unpredictable and often not immediately visible. But if we look carefully, we can see them in our own backyard—the Watsonville Sloughs.

MAP OF WEST STRUVE SLOUGH

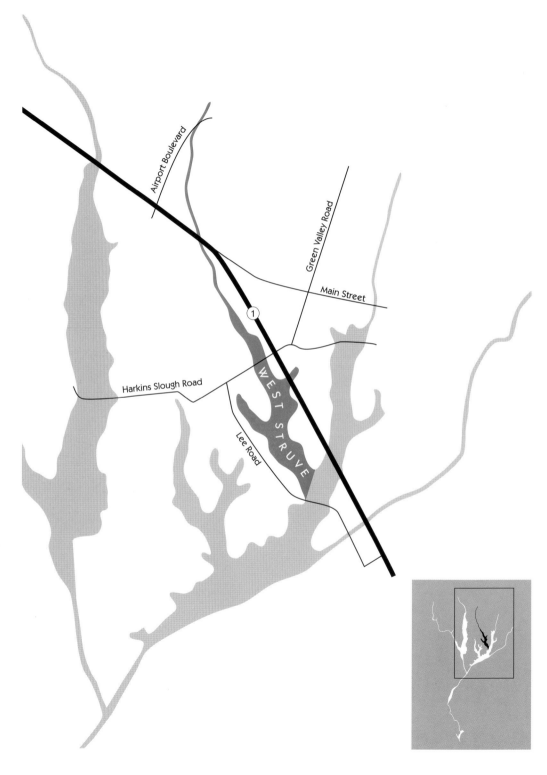

Airport Boulevard

Green Valley Road

Main Street

1

Harkins Slough Road

Lee Road

WEST STRUVE

West Struve Slough

*West Struve Slough originates off Airport
Boulevard, crossing under Highway One near
Harkins Slough Road. It parallels Highway One
and Lee Road along its course to its juncture with
Struve Slough. It can be viewed from Harkins
Slough Road west of the Highway, and from Lee
Road. Visitors can also obtain permission from the
California Department of Fish and Game to
enter the Ecological Reserve between Lee Road and
the Highway.*

WATCHING THE WETLANDS

Out on West Struve Slough, in a pool no more than an acre in size, three pied-billed grebe families are growing. It has been a wet May and the slough is swollen with water, just how these minnow chasers like it. One of the families is quite conspicuous, even from my vantage point on the terrace top. A female grebe sits on a nest near the pool's west margin, while her mate cruises in long reaches back and forth across the open water, coming within a few feet of the nest on each pass.

This morning the slough is alive with activity. The red-winged blackbirds have moved out of the bulrushes that they favored last year into thickets of hemlock and fennel, the tall parsley relatives grown lush by the generous spring rains and a decade of protection from grazing. The birds vocalize boisterously and chase one another from home plots. A common yellowthroat pops up a few feet away from my observation point and whistles melodically as he eyes me, then departs. Marsh wrens and another yellowthroat or two raise a din in the marsh. Cliff, barn and violet-green swallows twitter in swarms. Goldfinches, stunning in plumage and music, parade back and forth on roller-coaster sojourns through the air. An anise swallowtail butterfly comes and goes.

After an hour of witnessing this show, I realize that another grebe is sitting on a nest straight down in front of me, half a football field away. Her drab olive coloration matches perfectly the dead stalks that make up her nest.

While I watch this second female, a ruddy duck paddles into view. Close behind him is a third mother grebe, maybe three-fifths his size, ushering the trespassing ruddy out of her territory. Then she abruptly turns around, throws back her head and hoots enormously. She dives at the base of a clump of tule reeds and quickly reappears with a black morsel, probably a tadpole. Her loitering half-grown young promptly snatch it from her beak. It's lunchtime, and the male grebe I first spotted cruising on the pond relieves his mate on the nest for thirty minutes. Soon the second female also gets a break, thanks to her mate, for about twenty minutes.

Having served his midday nest duty, the cruising male acts decidedly relieved. He stretches one lobed foot out over the water. He scratches his head. He preens for a good long while, pausing only to eye another male near the boundary between their territories. The female, meanwhile, lowers herself primly atop the nest and calmly commences another long shift.

As I watch the birds over a span of several hours, these short breaks are the only time-out from nest sitting these females enjoy. Short, intermittent meal breaks are evidently sufficient for the females to obtain the food they require to sustain themselves to perform their motherly duties. With deft, chicken-like beaks and superb eyesight, they dive into murky water and snag minnows that flicker by like bolts of aquatic lightning. As in all birds, the largest part of the brain is the cerebellum, which controls movement. The grebes' uncanny coordination is the evolutionary product of eons of fish chasing, and a miracle to watch.

I stand up slowly and wait for the marsh to react. A pair of gadwalls darts up, circles overhead and resettles as I slowly move away. A pair of cinnamon teal ducks flies behind the hill. Harassed by several blackbirds, a great gangly bittern performs an aerial U-turn at my flank and dives into some cattails.

Exiting, I stumble upon the nest of a mallard, or possibly a gadwall, the seven bluish-white eggs neatly opened at the narrow end and all the contents eaten out. Nearby, a blackbird nest, containing two eggs, has been torn down. The most likely culprits: raccoons, opossums, skunks, or rats—all of which live in abundance around the area's farms.

LOVE ON THE WING

Nature may be "red in tooth and claw," as Alfred Lord Tennyson wrote. But she is also possessed of a big, affectionate heart. A Valentine's Day sojourn into the slough found a group of us bird-watchers marveling at what we imagined to be unfettered ardor among the birds of the muck, although really, the dances we witnessed performed by the birds that day were elegant, subtle, and proper as a tea ceremony.

Psychologists tell us aggression and sex are kin, yet how they are related we have barely begun to fathom. At first glance it appears that yonder dive-bombing white-tailed kite is bent on punishment. But as we watch him, a surprise awaits us. The male kite flies over a choice willow perch, one decorated by the trappings of spring greenery. His mustard-yellow boots, usually tucked away like proper landing gear, droop tantalizingly beneath his striking white belly. His whistle is songlike, a call that sounds simultaneously yearning and full of assurance.

Then, courtship begins. He rises. A female is in the air as well, flying just below him and a bit to the side. They glide gently over the terrain, hardly moving. Abruptly, he dips. She rolls. They're as synchronized as Fred Astaire and Ginger Rogers. Their toes clasp and, backs to the earth, they begin spinning, falling to a point just above the ground, where they fly apart. The male returns to his perch, but after a short while he rises again. A third bird has—deliberately, it appears—crossed into his domain. He flies straight after it. The interloper loses ground rapidly but makes it to the invisible border of the male's territory.

The mating later is as easy as falling off a log. Without any preliminary moves, the male steps on to the female's back, and they unite for a few (rapturous?) moments, then separate. They rest quietly. A gray harrier hawk passes by, working the narrows of the little hill, a sad remnant of the wide grasslands that only within the last decade have crumbled before a succession of disc harrows, bulldozer blades, and augers. The harrier is not likely to find a mate here this season and stay. Not far off, a pair of red-tailed hawks shares a telephone pole over

a prime patch of hunting ground. Perhaps their courtship—with the stunning stoop by the male just inches from a back-rolling female—occurred earlier in the day, unnoticed by us. In a willow near the peat pond, another pair of red-tails sits close together, so perfectly aligned that the pair silhouettes as one.

SEASON OF RAPTORS

In September the hawks come in. They arrive at the sloughs before the ducks and shore-birds, for they do not need to wait for the rains. They blow down from the north on the first blusters of foul weather and continue to arrive for most of the winter, their numbers depending on abundance of voles and squirrels and how the mood swings of civilization happen to be treating them that year.

You can feel hawks in the wind. You'll be out on a terrace and a freshet of marine air will blow hair in your eyes and you'll look up at the walls of great gray cumulonimbus clouds piling up in the wet air. Down across the cloud front will glide a red-tailed hawk, necklace and wrist patches darkly vivid against its creamy breast and wings. A few breeding pairs of red-tails have been there all summer, of course, but come winter there will be five to twenty on any given day, and they will usually be the first hawks you'll see. Your second raptor sighting might be a red-shouldered hawk, hunkered down in an apple tree in the orchard, red epaulets gleaming in the low light. Before long it'll disappear into the grass and rise with a vole.

Along the slough borders, in the willows, or sometimes soaring with the red-tails, will be swift pigeon hawks, or merlins, as well as Cooper's and sharp-shinned hawks. They are there to prey on huge flocks of finches and sparrows feasting on the big seed clusters that ripen on dock and smartweed plants during autumn and winter. The merlin will first appear as a small grayish blur. He will rocket by ground-feeding birds and as they spray, panic-stricken, up into

the air, he'll snatch one with rapier talons, and vanish. The long-tailed Cooper's and sharp-shinned hawks prefer to launch ambushes from the trees.

Watch carefully the red-tailed hawks' gyres. Many are the days that a large, flat-winged golden eagle or a rare rough-legged or ferruginous hawk joins in the wide, circling flights. These "buzzard hawks," so named for their habit of spending indolent hours soaring on set wings, terrorize ground squirrels that establish colonies along the sides and terrace ends of the sloughs. But the hawks are essential to a healthy slough ecosystem. Without hawks, the rails, ducks, herons, avocets, and other bird species that breed in the sloughs would rapidly succumb to predators such as skunks, raccoons, opossums, foxes and weasels.

Hunting these ground predators, the hawks limit the predators' consumption of the wetland birds. Big sprawling housing developments affect this delicate balance, disturbing the hawks, reducing their habitat and pushing them out of the land around the sloughs. At the same time, new housing increases populations of house cats, dogs, and Norway rats—also predators of native wildlife. To save the sloughs, you must save the uplands, realm of the raptors.

MAP OF WATSONVILLE SLOUGH

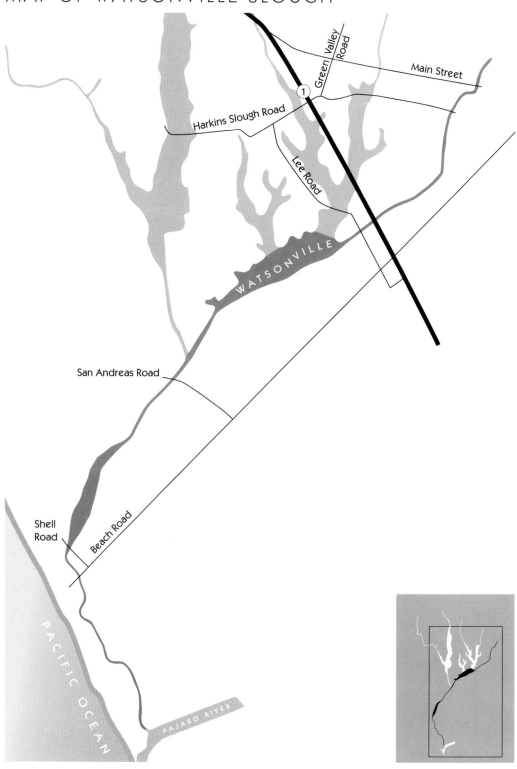

Green Valley Road

Main Street

1

Harkins Slough Road

Lee Road

WATSONVILLE

San Andreas Road

Shell
Road

Beach Road

PACIFIC OCEAN

PAJARO RIVER

Watsonville Slough

While for much of its course Watsonville Slough appears to be little more than a drainage ditch, it is in fact the backbone of the system that drains the rest of the sloughs. It includes several important wetlands at its upper reaches. From its origin along Ramsay Park in Watsonville, Watsonville Slough passes under Main Street and Harkins Slough Road and thence under Highway One, Lee Road, and San Andreas Road. It is pumped into the lower, tidal reaches at Shell Road and flows under Beach Road to join the Pajaro River at Monterey Bay. It can be viewed as a ditch paralleling Beach Road to the ocean, and as a tidal slough as it widens at Palm Beach.

LIFE ON THE EDGE

It is said there are no accidents in life; nowhere is this adage more true than out in nature, where the rules of ecology work in subtle ways that become visible only if you think about what you see.

Consider the hour's death: a vole run through by a marsh harrier's talons. No accident there—Greek tragedy all the way. The deceased was inexperienced and young, but wary. A little smaller than the other voles, he was forced by more dominant colony members into a sliver of habitat where, you observe, the grass is lower, the runways less developed, and forage sparser. Thus the vole had to travel farther from protection to find a meal. All these disadvantages added up to render this vole more vulnerable to an early death.

The hillsides provide wonderful, year-round habitat for a large number of voles, thanks to the nearby marsh, the seeps in the hillsides, and the clay sill within the soil that splits into deep, sheltering cracks. As for the marsh, it is there largely because of those same seeps, which wear away the terrace that feeds them and slowly forms the characteristic inroads of the Pajaro Valley, the sloughs.

Paradoxically, the ecology of the sloughs is fascinating partly because of human activity and the changes it has brought to the landscape. When grasslands were ploughed into orchards, field hawks declined in number. As orchards were left to decay, populations of goldfinches and linnets, drawn by unpicked fruit, flocked by the thousands, in turn attracting red-shouldered hawks, Cooper's hawks, merlins, and other bird hawks. Ground squirrels and gophers also multiplied and, as the trees thinned, voles increased too. The hawk population plummeted again when strawberry fields replaced orchard land and stands of thistle, fennel, and hemlock were demolished along the slough edges.

In the cycles of human activity occurring on these farmlands, the hope remains that some-day land can be acquired and returned to the more natural pattern of seasonal change. This unique, rare coastal, freshwater wetland-upland system deserves preservation. Urban development, of course, removes any hope of that. Like the vole that lived and died on the margin of its habitat, and indeed all the life forms that thrive in the overlapping edges of water and land comprising the wetlands, the Watsonville Sloughs are poised on an edge between extermination and survival.

What We Stand To Lose

I n a small alcove of West Struve Slough, the glint of a shoveler duck's plumage, beaming like reflector tape, catches my eye from a vantage point on Harkins Slough Road. Belonging to a flock of more than twenty, the bird is engaged in a swimming dance with a female, and the two are spinning in neat circles like the label of a phonograph record. Each time the male circles, the brilliant white and chocolate brown feathers along his side blaze preternaturally beneath the glowering sky. Within moments, two other couples join in, the spinning pairs resembling whirligigs in the quiet pool.

Nearby, two hooded mergansers vie for the attention of a female. Their shocking crests—among the most dramatic in the avian world—are unfurled like Spanish fans, and the fans' white patches blink like signal mirrors. The female leads them off in a quick nuptial chase. The several coots putzing about pay no attention to this activity, but a pair of gadwalls, another marsh duck, watches. A brief illumination by the sun unfettered by clouds, blows over. The slough dims as though someone had pulled a lamp cord, and the bird displays cease.

I mosey a few hundred yards along the road to the Hanson Slough overlook. Water flowing into upper Hanson has backed up behind a willow-studded berm, built by folks from the California State University–Monterey Bay Watershed Institute to trap excess sediment. A hundred mallards are floating on puddles or standing in them, while a great egret stares at the water pooling at his feet. A white-tailed kite campaigns across the slough, talons down, toward a mate perched atop an apple tree. The sun struggles through again, and a chorus of birdcalls erupts from the bottomland: yips and conkarees from the redwings, twits from the Audubon's warblers, and a stream of whistles from previously unannounced green-winged teal. Such vocal outbursts often herald a break in the weather.

In recent years it has been three freshwater sloughs—West Struve, Hanson and Harkins—rather than nearby College Lake or the tidally fed Elkhorn Slough that attracted the largest number of waterfowl in the region. Though many times larger than the Watsonville Sloughs, Elkhorn Slough is a salt marsh full of pickleweed and worms—wonderful for shore-birds but not so appetizing for waterfowl.

In contrast, the Watsonville Slough System is one of the largest freshwater marshlands left in California's coastal zone and one of the few remaining peat bogs. Teeming with meadow voles, ground squirrels, and other rodents, the sloughs represent the most important raptor habitat in Santa Cruz County. They also support a variety of rare breeding and wintering bird species, whose numbers have dwindled as development slowly encroaches. Land development around the sloughs decimates wetland wildlife in two ways: It destroys grassland habitats necessary for the survival of many species during periods of winter flooding, and it fosters conditions for predators of wetland animals to thrive and increase in number.

Loss of major parts of the slough system also represents a tragedy for future residents of Pajaro Valley, the whole of which growth threatens to urbanize within a very few decades. The disappearance of the sloughs impacts the region and the state, too. California has already lost more than 99 percent of its freshwater wetlands, and many of the associated species along with them. Can we afford to lose any more?

ECOLOGY OF THE URBAN FRINGE

The ecology of urban development is dismal. The effects of urban development along a slough boundary include:

⚘ The proliferation of house cats, Norway rats, skunks, and raccoons— all of which multiply and prey heavily on birds, resulting in the decimation of native bird populations in the slivers of natural habitat between slough and residences.

⚘ Back yards are extended and "escape" toward the marsh, introducing invasive alien plants.

⚘ The activities of humans and pets trample understory habitat and introduce litter.

⚘ Voles, a source of food for many raptors, lose their upland habitat and disappear.

⚘ Ground squirrels are squeezed into tiny spaces or eliminated, along with eagles and big hawks.

⚘ Hawks, lacking prey and habitat, move on.

⚘ The soggy upland hillsides are paved over, eliminating earthworms and, in turn, the herons and wintering shorebirds that stalk the hillsides for them.

⚘ Frequent disturbance and the proximity of houses reduce the use of the marsh by waterfowl.

⚘ The habitat is broken into pieces too small to support most species or provide protection from cats and similar predators.

⚘ Nesting and wintering habitats in upland areas no longer exist, so the myriad species that require them disappear.

Bird Species List

The following list of birds may reasonably be expected in our coastal sloughs. Those listed with an asterisk can be expected to be sighted uncommonly. It is not intended to be a definitive list; check with local bird clubs for rarities or unusual sightings. Names in all capitals, italicized, introduce a family or group of birds, e.g., *GREBES*; names in all capitals, not italicized, e.g., COMMON LOON, are the only representative of their family or group.

———————

COMMON LOON

GREBES
    Pied-billed Grebe
    Horned Grebe
    Eared Grebe
    Western Grebe
    Clark's Grebe

PELICANS, CORMORANTS
    American White Pelican
    Brown Pelican
    Double-crested Cormorant

HERONS, BITTERNS
    American Bittern
    Great Blue Heron
    Great Egret
    Snowy Egret

Cattle Egret
Green Heron
Black-crowned Night Heron

WATERFOWL
    *Greater White-fronted Goose
    *Snow Goose
    *Ross' Goose
    Brant
    Canada Goose
    Wood Duck
    Green-winged Teal
    Mallard
    Northern Pintail
    Blue-winged Teal
    Cinnamon Teal
    Northern Shoveler
    Gadwall
    Eurasian Wigeon

American Wigeon
Canvasback
Redhead
Ring-necked Duck
Greater Scaup
Lesser Scaup
Common Goldeneye
Barrow's Goldeneye
Bufflehead
Hooded Merganser
Common Merganser
Red-breasted Merganser
Ruddy Duck

HAWKS, FALCONS

Turkey Vulture
Osprey
White-tailed Kite
Northern Harrier
Sharp-shinned Hawk
Cooper's Hawk
Red-shouldered Hawk
Red-tailed Hawk
Ferruginous Hawk
Rough-legged Hawk
Golden Eagle
American Kestrel
Merlin
Peregrine Falcon
Prairie Falcon

CALIFORNIA QUAIL

RAILS, COOTS

Virginia Rail
Sora
Common Moorhen
American Coot

SHOREBIRDS

Black-bellied Plover
Semipalmated Plover
Killdeer
Black-necked Stilt
American Avocet
Greater Yellowlegs
Lesser Yellowlegs
Willet
Spotted Sandpiper
Whimbrel
Long-billed Curlew
Marbled Godwit
Ruddy Turnstone
Red Knot
Sanderling
Western Sandpiper
Least Sandpiper
Pectoral Sandpiper
Dunlin
Short-billed Dowitcher
Long-billed Dowitcher
Common Snipe
Wilson's Phalarope
Red-necked Phalarope

GULLS, TERNS

Bonaparte's Gull

Heermann's Gull

Mew Gull

Ring-billed Gull

California Gull

Herring Gull

Thayer's Gull

Western Gull

Glaucous-Winged Gull

Caspian Tern

Elegant Tern

Common Tern

Forster's Tern

Least Tern

Black Tern

PIGEONS, DOVES

Rock Dove

Band-tailed Pigeon

Mourning Dove

OWLS

Barn Owl

Great Horned Owl

Northern Pygmy Owl

*Burrowing Owl

*Long-eared Owl

*Short-eared Owl

SWIFTS, HUMMINGBIRDS

White-throated Swift

Anna's Hummingbird

Rufous Hummingbird

Allen's Hummingbird

BELTED KINGFISHER

WOODPECKERS

Acorn Woodpecker

Red-breasted Sapsucker

Nuttall's Woodpecker

Downy Woodpecker

Hairy Woodpecker

Northern Flicker

TYRANT FLYCATCHERS

Olive-sided Flycatcher

Pacific-slope Flycatcher

Western Wood-Pewee

Black Phoebe

Say's Phoebe

Ash-throated Flycatcher

Western Kingbird

HORNED LARK

SWALLOWS

Tree Swallow

Violet-green Swallow

N. Rough-winged Swallow

Bank Swallow

Cliff Swallow

Barn Swallow

JAYS, CROWS
- Steller's Jay
- Scrub Jay
- American Crow
- Common Raven

CHICKADEES, BUSHTITS
- Chestnut-backed Chickadee
- Plain Titmouse
- Bushtit

PYGMY NUTHATCH

BROWN CREEPER

WRENS
- Bewick's Wren
- House Wren
- Winter Wren
- Marsh Wren

KINGLETS, THRUSHES
- Ruby-crowned Kinglet
- Blue-gray Gnatcatcher
- Western Bluebird
- Swainson's Thrush
- Hermit Thrush
- American Robin
- Varied Thrush
- Wrentit

MIMIC THRUSHES
- Northern Mockingbird
- California Thrasher

AMERICAN PIPIT

CEDAR WAXWING

LOGGERHEAD SHRIKE

EUROPEAN STARLING

VIREOS
- Cassin's Vireo
- Hutton's Vireo
- Warbling Vireo

WOOD WARBLERS
- Orange-crowned Warbler
- *Nashville Warbler
- Yellow Warbler
- Yellow-rumped Warbler
- Black-throated Gray Warbler
- Townsend's Warbler
- Palm Warbler
- MacGillivray's Warbler
- Common Yellowthroat
- Wilson's Warbler

WESTERN TANAGER

GROSBEAKS, SPARROWS
    Black-headed Grosbeak
    Lazuli Bunting
    Spotted Towhee
    California Towhee
    Chipping Sparrow
    Savannah Sparrow
    Fox Sparrow
    Song Sparrow
    Lincoln's Sparrow
    Swamp Sparrow
    White-throated Sparrow
    Golden-crowned Sparrow
    White-crowned Sparrow
    Dark-eyed Junco

BLACKBIRDS, ORIOLES
    Red-winged Blackbird
    Tricolored Blackbird
    Western Meadowlark
    Yellow-headed Blackbird
    Brewer's Blackbird
    Brown-headed Cowbird
    Hooded Oriole
    Bullock's Oriole

FINCHES
    Purple Finch
    House Finch
    Pine Siskin
    Lesser Goldfinch
    Lawrence's Goldfinch

American Goldfinch

HOUSE SPARROW

Plant Species List

The following list of riparian and wetland plants can reasonably be expected to be seen in the Watsonville sloughs. It is not intended to be a definitive list.

Common name	Latin name
Bee-plant, California	*Scrophularia californica*
Blackberry, California	*Rubus vitifolius*
Bracken Fern	*Pteridium aquilinum*
Brass Buttons	*Cotula coronopifolia*
Brooklime, American	*Veronica americana*
Bulrush, Alkali	*Scirpus robustus*
Bulrush, Panicled	*Scirpus microcarpus*
Bulrush, California (Tule)	*Scirpus californicus*
Bulrush, Common (Tule)	*Scirpus acutus*
Bulrush, Olney's	*Scirpus olneyi*
Bulrush, Three Square	*Scirpus americanus*
Buttercup, Creeping	*Ranunculus repens*
Bur Reed	*Sparganium eurycarpum*
Cattail, Common	*Typha latifolia*
Cattail, Narrow-leaf	*Typha angustifolia*
Cocklebur	*Xanthium strumarium*
Cucumber, Wild	*Marah fabaceus*
Dodder	*Cuscuta salina*
Dogwood, Creek	*Cornus stolonifera*
Elderberry, Blue	*Sambucus mexicana*
Fat Hen	*Atriplex triangularis*

German Ivy, Cape Ivy	*Delairea odorata*
Gumplant	*Grindelia sp.*
Hazelnut, California	*Corylus cornuta californica*
Hemlock, Poison	*Conium maculatum*
Honeysuckle, Hairy	*Lonicera hispidula*
Horsetail	*Equisetum sp.*
Indian Hemp	*Apocynumn cannibinum*
Jaumea	*Jaumea carnosa*
Marigold, Bur	*Bidens laevis*
Marsh Pennywort	*Hydrocotyle ranunculoides*
Monkey Flower	*Mimulus guttatus*
Monkey Flower, Bush	*Mimulus aurantiacus*
Mugwort	*Artemisia douglasiana*
Nettle, Hedge	*Stachys bullata*
Nettle, Stinging	*Urtica holosericea*
Oak, Coast Live	*Quercus agrifolia*
Pickleweed, Common	*Salicornia virginica*
Plantain, English	*Plantago lanceolata*
Poison Oak	*Toxicodendron diversilobum*
Polypody	*Polypodium californicum*
Pondweed	*Potamogeton foliosus*
Radish, Wild	*Raphanus sativa*
Reed, Giant	*Arundo donox*
Rose, California wild	*Rosa californica*
Rush, Brown headed	*Juncus phaeocephalus*
Rush, Baltic	*Juncus balticus*
Rush, Bog	*Juncus effusus*
Rush, Common	*Juncus patens*
Rush, Toad	*Juncus bufonius*
Rush, Western	*Juncus occidentalis*
Ryegrass, Creeping wild	*Elymus triticoides*
Salt Bush, Australian	*Atriplex semibaccata*

Salt Grass	*Distichlis spicata*
Seaside Heliotrope	*Heliotropium curassavicum*
Sedge, Santa Barbara	*Carex barbarae*
Sedge, Slough	*Carex schottii*
Sedge, Wooley	*Carex lanuginosa*
Sneezeweed	*Helenium puberulum*
Smartweed, Lady's-thumb	*Polygonum persicaria*
Smartweed, Swamp	*Polygonum coccineum*
Smartweed, Water	*Polygonum punctatum*
Smartweed, Water-pepper	*Polygonum hydropiperoides*
Smartweed, Willow	*Polygonum lapathifolium*
Snowberry	*Symphoricarpos rivularis*
Spike-rush	*Eleocharis macrostachya*
Tarplant	*Holocarpha macrodenia*
Toyon	*Heteromeles arbutifolia*
Twinberry	*Lonicera involucrata*
Water Buttercup	*Ranunculus aquatilis*
Water Parsley	*Oenanthe sarmentosa*
Watercress	*Rorippa nasturtium-aquaticum*
Water Plantain, Common	*Alisma plantago-aquatica*
Willow, Arroyo	*Salix lasiolepis*
Willow, Red	*Salix laevigata*
Willow, Sandbar	*Salix hindsiana*
Willow, Yellow	*Salix lasiandra*

To order this book
from Watsonville Wetlands Watch

Send a check for	$12.95
shipping and handling	$ 2.00
California sales tax (8%)	$ 1.04
	$15.99

to: Watsonville Wetlands Watch
P.O. Box 1239
Freedom, CA 95019-1239